LEVIS CORNER HOUSE

Levis Corner House

Partridge Boswell

SOUTHWORD*editions*

First published in 2024
by Southword Editions
The Munster Literature Centre
Frank O'Connor House, 84 Douglas Street
Cork, Ireland

Set in Adobe Caslon 11pt

ISBN 978-1-915573-12-4

Contents

To kin of West Cork and every home to the nomad heart

THE STONE COTTAGE

—for Sarah

sits tacit as a tomb, quieter than noise-cancelling headphones
        on a windless pandemic afternoon that can only think of itself
and so opts not to think. The owners are away but left a note.

Walk in, latch the door, and you've stoppered time. Nothing gets
        in or out, save smoke from a basket of black turf by the hearth.
From that refurbished famine farm perched too cliff-high to hear

rollers roar below, you can see Fastnet tacked to the horizon
        and Cape Clear where once birders sighted a vagabond bobolink
blown clear across the pond. As a rule, stones will sing, though

these lie silent as the she-hare we spied our first morning
        crouched like a doorstop nibbling dew grass under the hedge,
so still she disappears when you blink. Stone mute as devoted

oath keepers sworn to archive windward sighs of luck and loss,
        joy and woe—stone thick as hay bales quarried from a gone time
before ignorance and thought-light engulfed the barren land

with furze yellow and rueful as Athenry, benign and lovely
        to look at until you slipped and fell into a copse of it crossing
the moor. Then, you found other names for it. That day we fell

into a new rhythm old as a *fulacht fiadh*, resisting an urge to leap up
        and run outside every time sun's face appeared like a neighbor
at the window—begging sugar, offering jam, expecting tea.

No urgency. She'd be back in a moment, and again tomorrow.
        Come morning, a pale horse grazing the slope across the road,
horizon in every direction. We folded our secrets and left them

beside a spray of hawthorn on the kitchen table. On cool wet days
        a thin braid of peat smoke threading the sea mist.
But only if you live in those parts.

Nor Easter

Do you know how her surgery went?
        What surgery? *She was supposed to have
a horse nebula removed from her head.*

There's that bright red bird again.
        *You know what they say about cardinals…
if you see one, that means a loved one has passed.*

I could play the fiddle all day long.
        Why don't you?
Might as well, naught else to craic.

…Seeds you bring me this Sunday morning
        in a month of Sunday mornings. They say it's
Easter, but obviously no bunny. Too Pythonesque—

all those fierce jellybeans and colored eggs
        and resurrection still over a month away
according to the Taoiseach's latest proclamation—

best the rabbit stay hid in his cave
        and we in ours till the gyre resets
& fret dissipates. You plant lilies in me—

superstition and odorless love tinged with
        fear bordering on laughter. If those slow
thighs could maybe speed the beast,

those indignant desert birds stop
        troubling my sight for just one day.
The falcon hasn't heard the falconer

in a long ass time. I'd give anything,
        my favorite song, for some of that fake
grass to remind me how we used to be.

WHITE HORSES

A pearl necklace round the neck of poverty
—Patrick Kavanagh

Promise posterity no empty bed, no monk-lit poem
            hidden in a cloud or rootbound rock, no golden
hour of sunrise or set. Some days, mountains are

mountains and silence a default yoke, phlegmatic
            as Beckett. Some days, noon's a giddy lad tramping
woods and fields, a dreamer in need of nothing

while shopkeeper cows ruminate in the abeyance
            between stomachs. Some days accidents happen
in threes, and the heart can't decide which to be

devastated by, so tears itself open to the wordless
            wind galloping in on the water's white horses
to where you stand naked on your promontory

of doubt, straining to see past a shifting horizon—
            a reason that may someday if not suss or justify
at least demystify the current calamity, so close

to absurdity you have to laugh out loud, Lear-like
            in the gale, the land's end there stripped of trees
as if living were a crime and time a white-sailed

sloop about to glide any moment into view
            cresting that crease of un/certainty—as you raise
your collar, wiping horse spit from your face.

Foraging

—*for Eavan Boland*

"It won't ever come to this—salivating at the sight
    of burdock and dandelions, tasting hawthorn's tender
lemony flavour when leaves are young, divining daisies

and wild violets, elder- and cuckoo flowers, muttering
    Yum! to none but your stomach, thrilled to discover
primrose strawberry sorrel, drooling at delicacies

of ubiquitous pookies, fruit of ancient wisdom blooming
    visions and medicinal tea from an unseen cosmos beneath
your feet. Somehow you'll be spared by the same *deus ex*

digitalis that swooped in and said *it could never happen here*—
    despite the fox and *gráinneog* who visit your porch, the deer
growing bolder, inching closer to help themselves to the house

garden now with your sentinel water spaniel gone; despite
    attention's dilation, lingering prayer-like in a prism's aura
the way ancient Greeks deified sun-rain in the goddess Iris.

You won't be told: the stores are all closed and you need
    to relearn the larder at arm's length like a lover right in front
of you, ready to be kissed. If only loose lips knew the use

of silence or tongues could dowse a gooseberry's dulcet succulence.
    The fire will never rise or rage hot enough to burn us back
to a virgin rebirth. What's lost is lost. We can't ever Hellenise

the island or be that close again, tightly woven in a warped
    weft, just another random animal in a zoo of its own design
where a name can't tame a living thing, and earth still defines

us without a word. We won't ever be Nora and her little sister—
    studying a bark beetle's cuneiform labyrinth, flight paths of lone
crows, and bottomless well-holes of barn owl eyes, while signs

recalibrate to dreams, not to be talked about, but *realised*—
out foraging their wild food salad in backyard copse and glen
in a singsong litany of ripe surprises, reviving our lost gift,

kenning in a glimpse and whiff what's edible and what isn't…"
Or so you say to a basket of fiddleheads you set on a lichened
rock to savour the tuning orchestra of day-blind stars above.

WALLFLOWERS

A plea went out via local social media—
i.e. tea and vegan sausage rolls at Budd's,
flower shop alstroemeria, the ladies morning
swimming club at Audley Cove, and slipped

like a black toucan between reliable pints
of FC and GAA play-by-play at Levis'—for
volunteers to help revive the community hall.
In a desilvered mirror you can see yourself:

coveralled, paint and brush in hand, smartening
up cinder block walls, or tidying the charity shop
upstairs, pairing a needed item with its new owner
like the village match-maker, soliciting donations

from Land Rover summer folk… or breathing through
a tai chi tiger or pretzeled yoga pose, or just as readily
minding the annual car boot sale… or on the phone to that
bindlestiff theater troupe whose uncensored bedroom wit

kept eyes fixed, tongues wagging, ears stitched and
mill-monger Eimear O'Mahony blogging endless
craic for a week in high season… and wouldn't Colm
and Eoin want to get the band back together again

to revisit those Pogues and Saw Doctors covers?
and draw us all from the shadows of our shuttered
walls where we're plastered on a Morris floral print
twitching in our Sunday best, studying each other's

faces across the hall, thinking how much easier this
all was only a year or two ago when we were kids—
how we wouldn't even be here if it weren't for the music—
tapping along wondering when the next song will be ours.

Upon Hearing Amy Winehouse at St. James' Church in Dingle

Grief without song could be any stone chapel built of loss
packed with aging villagers lulled reticent as rue
by a rote bell's tongue, hemmed by iron gates and a yew
tree lurking mirthlessly beside a burial ground where moss-

patinaed saints and earth angels gather round relic icons
of threadbare hand-me-down faith. You sit/kneel/stand on
your misericord, an eaten Job in the organ belly's drone,
sorting your parents' hoarded aggregate—clothes pawn

and charity shops won't take, sewing kits, boxes of old
Polaroids of anonymous sepia-people you wouldn't be here
without, file drawers of past taxes, uniforms from the war,
wedding dress, unworn shoes unfit for a holy soul…

—and that's just the tip, to say nil of unspeakable sins
in attic and basement. Macular shorebirds scan whitecaps
for questions the mind's eye can alight: dim synapse
of a candlelit nave, musty kneelers, a deacon's

chair from Suriname. Grief without song is wasted pain.
According to patron James, *faith in works*—in real acts
of creation—amplifies our part in salvation's soundtrack
louder than wafers, wine or words of mumbled expiation

dissolved on penitent tongues. In your rusted anechoic
husk, your veins blood-thrum a rushing river-hymn,
an electric fence of nerves ticking in your cerebellum—
until silence clears its throat… and from her first chthonic

tremolo it comes as no shock: how from Galway to Summerhill
churches are being repurposed as concert halls by clergy who swear
love's lost call note still lingers, runic under the moored murmur
of all those services you sat unmoved through, the supernal

flatulence of organ bellows at last revised in fidelity rare
as a black velvet angel with spindly legs and mental hair,
her aqueous blues beguiling as the B-side of prayer
beside an ocean we couldn't hear but always knew was there.

WATERWISE

—An de bheoaibh no de mhairbh thu?

You never liked the ocean, its cloying brine and vertiginous

    mystery of open water. The week it took to sail from Brooklyn

        to Southampton you nearly opened your wrists—trapped with

            in-laws in a seasick spate of endless green-faced buffets

        and waterboard pretense, when you could have flown in hours

    and explored all of Cornwall and Devon by the time they docked.

Waterwise, you preferred your family's sand-spit on the southern Gulf

    where you'd wade in warm aquamarine's acquiescence and welcome

        even stingrays and barracuda, danger losing its dubious credentials

        in that bright translucence. You loved its calm bathtub clarity

    so much, we scattered some of you in your favorite inlet there

    where fresh and salt comingle at the mangroves' mouth. Some here,

some there—funny how you're no- and everywhere in the same wink.

    Freed from panic boxes, we go looking for you now in the Azores

        or Seychelles or the pond next door, trailing whale song and pods

        of dolphins in our glass bottom boat, exploring psychedelic coral

    and unrequited anemones waving in the waterlight. Last night

between my heart's hidden spring and honeycomb, I dreamed we were caravanning beside a raw Gaeltacht coast. Without dipping

a toe, you were the first to dive from dark rocks, dripping sleek as

a svelte selkie, beckoning us to follow you into a cold cobalt

abyss. You know best how this next swell rolls: connection's

deferred return, treading out over our heads to reconnect us with

what's already connected. How we're supposed to unfold and

unfurl ourselves, as last night's white horses scatter a red tide.

The Coast Guard declares the sea safe again, and we can look

each other in the beacons of our eyes and for the first time actually

see someone else beyond our own craggy shore—faces risen close

to the harbor's surface, gorgeous and terrifying as the Man-o-War

we spied bobbing off Bantry pier, which proved to be just a compass

jelly, common as one of Rilke's angels, flashing in the shallows.

THE BATHERS

—for Juliana Macleod

Strolling to Audley Cove under a low ceiling of cloud,
the cool dull torpor trying to pass for a day's shadow
presumes you'll sit alone on the pebbly strand till a wave-
less gray lapping of solitude pervades… *when what's this?:*

a carnival of Saltimbanques—swim-costumed families and
wee ones in floaties, carpools and vans of them pulling up
to the hidden inlet in droves like it's high summer, not nearly
October. Mothers asking brightly: *Have you been swimming yet?*

It's lovely! Kids shouting and splashing, surrounding cliffs
resounding with family palaver and laughter. What kind of
Weetabix did they eat for breakfast? you wonder, to convince
themselves a bleak mid-week morning is everyday's holiday—

that the numbing water's a tropical turquoise, the gray pebbles
silken as virgin sand, that the showerheads are real and all will
be well and cleansed in the room they've been told to shower in,
having done as the uniformed Fräulein instructed and memorized

the number of the peg on which they hung their clothes so they
could retrieve them after bathing… that things indeed are looking
up after so long and hard a journey. And now turning to slip jig
the bee-loud road home, haven't they convinced you as well?

NEW WORLD

I'm in the back of the bus with Seamus
   giving him a tour of the new theme park,
and all he wants is to straighten the round-

abouts south of Tralee. The theme being
   civilization: *sardinhas* packed in sunlight
one on top of another tight as Rio's *favelas*,

except all the construction—from shanties
   & shrines to palaces & slapdash cathedrals—
is new, not a mote of calamity's landscaping

or suffering's lawn to buffer shared plywood
   walls, their spotless facades empty of spiritual
possibility. Through the caravan window I

point out his beloved Sandymount strand, sand-
   wiched between Alhambra and Machu Picchu,
Timbuktu minarets and the cloisters at Melk.

When are we stopping? a green Seamus
   wants to know, the accuracy of theme park
gods failing to impress. His white brow fizzes;

cradling an ashplant, he only wants to hear
   if empirical proof of nine dimensions gives us
hope of heaven. A new world elides into view

and finally we stop. He steps off and bokes.
   I haul his luggage out from below. *Forget
the bags*, he says laying aside uilleann pipes

to pick up a pennywhistle. *Let's see
   what all this seafóid is about.*

GLOSSARY OF THE BOTTOM LINE

Spreadsheet is what covers the bed or newly dead
who have no need for breath or bread, or tallies of toys
or estate taxes or eye-penny platitudes a eulogist just read.

Amortization is both loving and dying—entropy's slow
return to nothing without even trying. Have you conducted
a full audit of your heart's conduct? Your *book value*

depends not simply on the cover's depreciation but
the compounding interest in its pages. Untaxable wages
and fungible widgets consigned to bad credit; wheat

and chaff assets fixed or sifting a stiff wind for *kiting*—
a check bouncing down an empty street rubbery
as a ball you once lost when you were three

or was it four? Abacus, craps and beans… p&l, budget,
aging, ends and means… counting beats in Talking Heads'
I Zimbra… Play or dread it, you're in a zero-sum game

of debit & credit, gross & net: graft's swift enjamb
ment once you accrue such height, your mid
floor suite tawdry as a refugee encamp

ment. Readjusting your top line, give your planned
obsolescence scheme a tweak, a discrete embezzle
ment to cement your ascent, and Ponzi-neat finesse

the penultimate leap to the penthouse, your enrich
ment writing off the risk of your inevitable empoor
ment. Once gained, you can't say what the 88th floor

meant or the net purpose of your employ
ment, aside from transposing congealed energy,
fiddling with others' numbers to color your dream

of furnishing empty houses in Jackson Hole
and Pumpkin Key, your former assets now
liabilities of cloned desire and worry.

Liquidity alas is something you won't share with those
in or outside your gated community; an ability to manumit
slaves of debt, to make amends, reparations and reconciliations—

to see a life as solvent, portfolio holdings notwithstanding,
hands not asking for handouts but raised in unison, share-
holders in the same public company as the vaquita and black-

footed ferret, casting ballots for taxing the truly taxable,
for safe schools and capitols, like the one in that small island
country with the modest GDP whose large-hearted people

will give you their bootstraps and sleeves to break even,
whose pot is always full and glittering with eudaimony
because their *capital* is always Dublin.

SLÁN ABHAILE

…the young people trapped in their destinies
like caged animals out of touch with their instinct
—Cathal Ó Searcaigh

You notice it most in the liberated silence of his absence—
a month's hibernation stretched to years of living in his head,
his heavy sigh of abeyance, off to the lake on holiday with friends,
your tact wearing thin—how desperately he needs to shake the fold,

slip the comfortable creature skin of his avatar and wander unenhanced
by infinite RAM and a hundred PPI monitor. After abandoning plan
after plan by the roadside, he needs to cut and run without one—
before his one wild and precious life atrophies to a gaming hand,

his limitless possibilities stagnating in paralytic pretexts
for never having to leave, twitching on the shoulder of a quiet
country lane waiting for real danger's rare vehicle to whoosh next
to almost past before dashing across harm's way. And maybe he's legit

in wondering: *Will the world ever be safe again?* But maybe you need
to answer less gently: *When was it ever to those who refuse to release*
their own captors, or to till and plant and water their own seed?
You thank his friends and beg them: *Come again, soon. Please.*

MY LUCKY DAY

was the day we met—though who can say
      when that was? Dim, inauspicious at best,
did the occasion occur in the wan tepid

slant of incidental socially-distanced friends,
      a paper partition Zen monks hung between
our shadow-voices? Here in fate's vestibule I can

only attend thought's current school. How many
      lives do we idly cut & paste before arriving at love?
Who can say if this morning's faithful, pecking

the rain-soaked lawn, are juncos or wrens? Are we
      more than an accident of tense? How many runs did
we lug the implausible luge back up the mountain

to find the perfect line down the track—not too high
      or low, slow or fast—the optimal flow of gravity,
celerity and trajectory winding from *No* to *Perhaps*

to the soul's silent assent, inexorable as the lingua
      franca of our dovetailed gaze, the Yes in our eyes
hot enough to liquefy ice? In your repeating dream

you liberate vivid glimpses from refugee sleep—
      a train station or apartment above a cobbled street,
a farm's wooded edge—always the tensile sense

of an urgent plot unfolding across countries
      and centuries, always the river of night to cross,
the tree-lined road that leads me back to you.

How many dress rehearsals do we need to grow
      into the role that creates us as we speak, their fleet
flaws sending audiences packing so we can share

the stage free of drama and scripts, with only
    a lingering ghost light for saying it comes to this:
I could kiss you forever... And if that isn't kismet

I taste on your lips, let me be the Lucky Dip winner
    of the Ballydehob Lotto on a week no jackpot's won—
my ticket fished from a trashcan cradled by the Lord

Mayor's hand—not waiting endlessly for our numbers
    to tumble into place, but turning to the child in you
beside me now, the lost friend found.

THE POET'S WAY

—Sheep's Head, West Cork

…wends from walled paddocks through a mute glen of sea grass curried
      by ceaseless susurration gleaning secrets from a pentameter of countless
steps who've passed here one to the next… and by the time you reach

the lighthouse and peer into a tidal crevasse where three girls drowned
      a century ago and so added their names to the cliffs' brutal beauty…
and see the stray lamb suckling his stray mother where the land ends

and wonder how sheep could wander so far in a shepherd's dream
      and what moved people to farm such rocky desolate slopes where
wind tears at mandrake roots, and why still they try—unless perhaps

the gale's plaintive howl reminds them every moment to joyfully toss
      their entire life into the scales of fate… and by the time you pass a small
shrine tucked into the cliffside—Our Lady of the Wayside—her open

arms and beatific gaze imparting succoring grace to any wayward
      traveler in need of rest or strength, plodding hungrily up to the car
park's stone café to brave the tour bus crowd after communing all

day with metaphysics of wind and sea—the solitary self, a high cairn
      set in stark relief against the sky… straining, reaching out to touch
what's either light in god's face or the backside of just another cliché,

before your soul can get its bearings and shrink… you leave their safe
      complacent numbers behind to amble final miles on legs gone slack,
your sun- and salt-lashed face glowing transfigured by forces no mill

or pen can harness, your spirit untamable and wild as white horses
      galloping across the bay… it's impossible to say where exactly,
which view among hundreds, what beauty too breathless to be held

or loss too sad to retell, what stretch of rock or dirt or bog sacrificed
      itself to the gust that blew your heart open, which stile you clambered
over, meandering unmown fields of farms perennially on the edge of ruin,

trusting a well-trod thread as your head wandered aimless as a poet's cloud
     over landscapes real and imagined… fingering scales laden with the weight
of unshorn wool, turning your back on numbers and stones when the nurse

weighs you from birth until your last appointment's intake, every measuring
     up a gathering and scattering until even that staunch superstition fades
and falls away in the joyous mournful moan of your mother's selkie

voice drifting out with the tide. You toss your entire life in anyway,
     shattered and unrecognizable to anyone but you, burnished clean
of every bright path, tried or true, the fleet shadow of every thought.

An Irish Hello

We saw a neat trick at the Locke Bar in Limerick
whilst waiting for the nightly trad session to begin,

a stout man of impish ebullience blew into the crowded
public house and announced: *The greatest man in Ireland's*

*about to walk through this door! When he does, let him
know how much you love and cherish him! Here he comes…!*

and there we stood on the edge of our stools, tippling on
the rim of a buzz, aglow in unmasked company again

more alive than a good long while, if not our alivest ever,
the hushed room electric with anticipation… Is it Bono?

Michael Higgins? Roy Keane? Paul O'Donovan? Gabriel
Byrne? Liam Neeson? The Pope?… when an ordinary bloke

walks in (naive sidekick of a tick ago's jolly impresario)
to the roar of a hundred half-drunk idolaters working hard

with hands and mouths to give a run-of-the-mill Joe regular
as them a hero's welcome and celebrate his infinite acclaim

and legend—which is of course our own, the prank being
on none but us. Whereupon the man, smiling and waving

to his biggest fans and most ardent admirers, after soaking
it up, turns and heads back out the door and across the street

to have a quiet pint at a picnic table by the quay and
a word with the man who can only be his best friend.

First Snow

Spring, the sweet spring, was not sweet for us
Nor winter neither.
—Nuala Ni Dhomhnaill

Bound to memory, not a bowsprit of If. *I found that*
snowflakes were miracles of beauty wrote Wilson
Bentley, microscope poised for his Oracle's arrival.
Ghosts shook their robes last night, the lawn a thin

tarpaulin of lime dust. Invoke the word and winter
invites itself altarward. Mustn't let them take a picture
and steal your soul. Think of Marconi in his signal
station perch, the sea's contempt spitting against

Brow Head's ragged cliffs. Mustn't look at police
after your arrest. Maybe it never happened. Maybe
you and she were bound for each other ever since
that night at the Gare de l'Est, fleeing with a young

family clinging to your sides, back and breast,
throats frozen open with what might come next—
maybe you don't exist, and here's not here nor there
in a ticketless mist of transition to who knows where

not knowing separation's only ever a temporary station.
Oceans, mountains… are nothing to the burning road,
forbidden to the bidden, the hollow between waves.
Mustn't trust the azure foreshore at Barley Cove,

the cold fire of its lucid allure icy-hot enough to sterilize
a nuptial couple's midday tryst. You wetsuit up and swoon
into the abyss while blue-lipped children laugh more-or-less
buff for hours in the surf, lashed and happy as Larry.

ODE TO A POEM BEGGING TO BE A SONG

—after Patrick Kavanagh and Luke Kelly

A blue dirge worms into your urgent ear.
She turns to go, slipping unembraced down
a late autumn road into unfathomable shadow,
the sea of your longing bright as a rising moon

belied alone by the nightlight left on inside your
soul's dovecoat. Resigned to flow, you mount
crepuscular steps to Mrs. Kenny's boarding house,
content to pry stuck mussels from disenchanted

depths lifeless as an empty pint glass. Or so you
concede, yet how lasciviously its pageantry pulses!:
nudibranch and extemporaneous crustacean, butterfly
and clown fish weaving widdershins around a coral

labyrinth. A euphony of secret creatures fills you
past the brim with a warm anthropic honey-tone,
enticing unrequited clay to jig and rig a spinnaker's
luster of uptempo laughter—compelling the future

that devours us to back away from the table waving
its hands saying *Keep this bittersweetness if you must.*
Then maybe bees at least won't waltz so abstemious.
If it means so much, for gods' sake, just keep it.

are all writing about frost this morning. I have no clue
what their counterparts in Ghana are doing, but will bet
they're not word-painting hoared hedgerows bejeweled
with glass brambles, shamrock vales and ruby fuchsia

effaced by a sea of ice. Love's unlikely to get warmer
wherever poets aren't scribbling, singing as they swing
from treetops, cracking crazed enamel with shamanic
incantations—praising cold and heat alike for lighting

a fire under our backsides, spelling head- and heart-
lines no longer implying but crying out: Earth is now
under its own weather seeded by callow gods, i.e. us.
In Inniskeen, Jack the leprechaun's bestowed a name

because locals need some specific goat to shoulder
blame for such sweeping arctic mischief—like a dubbed
hurricane or telescope cruising deep space, whenever
destiny swerves to miss an *aos si* we didn't see.

Here, where anomaly alternately wears banality's ice-
caked beard, a poet pours a cup of black dawn, drags
her cigarette in waxing light. *I'll stay warm if it kills me*
she says to her boot soles squeaking over vestal snow

retrieving the morning paper for news she can erase,
to see if that madman is still on the loose. Not the one
you're thinking of… but that's okay, we get confused,
so many little Hitlers in tights, in Armani, in stone-

washed jeans. Evergreens sag under the page's white
weight. She turns to let the day melt a mother's tears,
heads back inside for warmth to color cold clarity,
her misted breath curling behind her like smoke.

Levis Corner House

A narrow tributary of road unravels past
        paddock and farm; an involuntary life funnels
into wasp-waisted streets of a harbor town.

Take as many pictures as you please, save as many
        souls. Pick an aster to keep between two leaves
of your favorite poem. This caravan has no rearview

to revisit sighs that might have been. You can only
        see up a rise down the road ahead. One by one
lights blink on in homes and shops as if to say

This can't be all—there must be more to this fading
        treacle of tidal spoor and famished child. Meet me
at the pink pub on the corner, half-past workday's end:

a side door you didn't see opens on a loved-one's
        vanishing cohabiting with your *Turas d'Anam*
where fiddle and bouzouki are warming—a word-

worn womb lilting with human music tuned
        to distance gradually diminished by intention
subsumed by a harmonium's flat drone,

harmony-sharpened into perfect pitch. Laugh
        we shall and tip a pint of *cairdeas* with Jung
in our illuminated room among all the people

to whom we belong in reality, toasting the irony
        of your journey that finds you and the weekend
finally angled in shared repose, here and nowhere

else, your ken alive and dancing to a convivial
        din, beside a stranger who loves you… and we
talk until last call never comes and every arrow

that murders sleep is broken… until we amble
        home arm-in-arm without ever leaving, praying
to the moon and stars in the burning churches

of our bodies without being singed. Behind us,
        a wordless choir swelling on the bodhrán
bones of that village, in its hale pink heart.

Ensō Carousel

One whirl, all music and bright color, wild horses and laughter
rutting a black circle, imperfect as π to a thousand reams of paper.

Over / under alternate faster until they blur into one current
and you ride the dun mare through a burning ring of gold.

In this life the most you can hope for is one or two friends
who won't mind if you love them. One or two durable

songs you never tire of singing and, for reasons unclear,
others never tire of hearing. One or two days drenched

with sun and rain that shouldn't but somehow add up
to a persistent glow you have no word for but *aoibhneas*.

One or two memories that haunt you like blue veins
of light you assumed were best bled and forgotten

yet deepen and feed you as they darken. One or two
songbirds you never see hidden inside the magnolia

who insist you name them according to their music.
One or two words of advice shirked long ago you're now

dying to impart to any fool who will listen. One or two
obsessions that burn in the distance—sacramental flames

of your next life. One or two lives crystalized into the salt
you needed to taste the one you're living. The most you

can hope for is one or two gifts disguised as strangers
who arrive well past midnight, who wake tomorrow

to bright canopies of wind-kissed light, see you dancing
in the highest branches, and decide to stay for breakfast.

Acknowledgements

Grateful acknowledgement is made to the editors, readers and judges of the following publications and venues in which versions of poems first appeared:

Fish Anthology: "The Stone Cottage"

Plume Poetry Journal: "Nor Easter"

Poetry: "Upon Hearing Amy Winehouse at St. James' Church in Dingle"

"The Stone Cottage" was selected for the 2022 Fish Flash Fiction Prize

"Upon Hearing Amy Winehouse at St. James' Church in Dingle" was selected for the 2020 Telluride Institute Fischer Prize (2nd)

"The Poet's Way" was selected for the 2022 Welsh International Poetry Prize (2nd)

My earnest thanks to all—named and unnamed—who had a hand in bringing these words to light and life: Aisling Roche, Donagh Long, Caroline O'Donnell, Joe O'Leary, Clem Cairns, Jula Walton, Juliana Macleod, Paul Casey, Eavan Boland, Dominic Taylor, Anatoly Kudryavitsky, Sheila Ryder, John Sexton, Kate Russell, Jon Carroll, Rebecca O'Connor, Simon Prim, Gerald Cosgrove, Michael Russell, Don Share, Danny Lawless, Tracey Slaughter and Mick Evans.

I'm especially and joyfully indebted to those who sustain the soundtrack of my creative life, most notably Peter Money, Nat Williams, my family, and my steadfast beacon, Sarah Rutledge.

Printed in Great Britain
by Amazon